A Kid's Book of First Aid:
Including the Official Junior Paramedic Test
and Official Junior Paramedic Card

ISBN **978-1503361034**

Printed in the United States of America

A Kid's Book Of First Aid

Including the
Official "Junior Paramedic" Test
and Official Junior Paramedic Card!

By Lance Hodge, Paramedic

I'm a Paramedic. I worked in the Fire Department on an ambulance. In an emergency I know what to do, and I'm going to teach you that.

What is an emergency?

An emergency is when something suddenly happens and somebody needs to do something quickly to help.

This book will get you ready to do the right thing in an emergency.

When you finish this book there's a test. If you can remember all these lessons you will know what to do in an emergency and you can pass that test! After you pass the test you will be an *Official Junior Paramedic*, wow!

3

So read this book carefully and try to remember what you've learned. When you finish you can tell your friends what you know and that you are now a *Junior Paramedic*.

If you miss any questions on the test you need to go back and study that page, and then go back and answer that question again. You need to get ALL the questions right, then you'll earn your *Official Junior Paramedic card.* Your parents will check your test to make sure you know all the right answers, and then they can cut out your card, put your name on it, and laminate it in plastic so that it will last a long time.

What is First Aid? Do you know?

First Aid is the FIRST thing you can do to try to fix some part of you or of somebody else that is hurt, or the thing you can do FIRST to help somebody who is sick and who might need a doctor.

Sometimes in an emergency people just don't know what to do. They might call 9-1-1 to get help but they don't know what else to do. You will learn what else to do to help the person who is hurt or sick while waiting for help to get there. When people don't know what to do sometimes they just cry or scream or run around, or sometimes they try to do *something* but it might be the wrong thing to do. If you do the wrong thing you might even make things worse.

This book will get you ready to do the *right thing.* We don't want to just scream or cry if something happens, we need to try to stay calm and DO something to help. You can cry about what happened later, but right when an emergency happens the *Junior Paramedic* needs to stay calm and think about the right thing to do. Cry later if you want to, that's

normal and that's ok, but first make sure you do the right things to help, and you'll learn all of that in this book.

Do you know what **common sense** is?

Common sense is when you know something is right or wrong even if nobody taught you that. Sometimes we just *know* that we shouldn't do something, because it seems dangerous, or because it seems wrong, or it just isn't a nice thing to do, and lots of times we know those things just because of *good common sense*. You should always try to use your good common sense, and if you think something isn't right then trust your common sense and don't do it. Our common sense can keep us safe if we trust it.

Sometimes an adult isn't home or an adult is having an emergency but *they* can't call 9-1-1. Sometimes something is wrong with a person and you can't wake them up. Sometimes they are breathing really weird, sometimes they just look very strange but can't talk to you. Your common sense tells you that they need help, and should call 9-1-1 right away. Stay calm, calling 9-1-1 is probably all you can do for them. After you call 9-1-1 help is on the way, they will come fast with their sirens on to help you. **Stay on the phone with the person at 9-1-1 unless they tell you to hang up the phone and do something else.**

Should you pet a strange dog you don't know just because it's wagging its tail? Your common sense probably tells you that you should NOT pet that dog, it just might bite, you never know. So trust your *common sense*.

Sometimes in an emergency there *is* something important we can do, but sometimes we can't really do anything that will help the problem, sometimes only the things a doctor can do will really help the problem.

If your common sense tells you that you really can't do anything to help, then just make sure you or somebody calls 9-1-1, **that is always the right thing to do in an emergency**.

The VERY FIRST thing we need to do in an emergency is to **make sure WE ARE SAFE**. If it seems like something dangerous is happening then we should stay away. Sometimes we can't try to help because it's just too dangerous. The EMT's and Paramedics and the Fire Fighters have special training in how to stay safe, and sometimes we just have to stay away and wait for them to help. But there is ALWAYS something really important we CAN do. **We can CALL for help, usually that means calling 9-1-1**. When we call 9-1-1 the person on the phone will be able to send help to our house, or to wherever you are. They can send the police if you need the police, they can send the fire department if you need the fire department, and they can send an ambulance if you need an ambulance.

A kid can call 9-1-1, you don't have to be an adult or get permission to call 9-1-1, if you think there is an emergency then **YOU** should call 9-1-1. And if something bad is happening to you but you don't know what to do about it, don't stay quiet, don't keep a secret about something that you know is wrong, you should call 9-1-1, they can get someone to help you, no matter what the problem is.

The people who can come to help when you call 9-1-1 can be EMT's, Paramedics, Fire Fighters, or Police Officers. An EMT is an *Emergency Medical Technician*, that's the First Aid training for people who work on ambulances and for Fire Fighters. EMT's and Paramedics usually drive an ambulance. A Paramedic has more training than an EMT, they have to go to a longer school to be a Paramedic, and they learn to do more things than an EMT can do. EMT's, Paramedics, and Fire Fighters all know how to do First Aid and can help people who are sick or hurt. People sometimes call the EMT's, Paramedics, and Fire Fighters that come to help, **rescuers**.

EMT's, Paramedics, and Fire Fighters know how to put on bandages for cuts, and splints for broken bones, and they have oxygen to help people breath. There is a LOT to learn to become an EMT or Paramedic and you have to study hard. When you are 18 years old you could take an EMT class at a college, some colleges have those classes, and when you pass all the tests you can work on an ambulance or sometimes in a hospital. Paramedics go to school longer than EMT's and also learn how to give shots and medicine and use special machines to see if a person's heart is beating like it should. If you want to be a Fire Fighter you also have to go to another school to learn all about fire equipment like fire trucks, hoses, ladders, saws, and other tools used by Fire Fighters.

EMT's, Paramedics, and Fire Fighters also learn how to do CPR and they learn what to do if someone is choking and how to use other special tools and equipment.

Here's what we're going to learn about:

What should you do if you get cut by glass or by something sharp?

What should you do if you have something sticking into you like a nail or a knife?

What should you do if you might have a broken bone?

What should you do if you get stung by a bee or wasp, or if you get bit by a dog or cat?

What is an infection?

What is an allergic reaction?

What should you do if you bump your head and now you have a big lump there?

What should you do if you get dirt or sand in your eyes?

What should you do if you get burned by something?

What should you do if you have trouble breathing?

What should you do if you have a bloody scrape on your skin from falling down?

What should you do if you get poison on you?

What should you do if your friend has a gun or a knife?

What should you do if your friend has drugs or wants you to use them?

That's a LOT of questions. We'll talk about all those things and even more. We'll talk about calling 9-1-1, using your shirt to stop bleeding, what you should do before help comes, and what to do if something seems dangerous to you.

Your test at the end of this book will be 15 questions, and you'll have to pay attention to what you read in this book to get the right answers.

When I talk about the answers to these questions I might say something like "What do you do if YOU have trouble breathing, or if YOU have a bump on your head, but I also mean what would you do if it happened to *somebody else*, it doesn't have to be YOU who got hurt or who is sick.

A Junior Paramedic should know what to do for *themselves* if THEY get hurt, but you also want to know what to do for someone else if some other person is hurt or sick. First Aid can be for yourself or for other people. It's really important to be able to help other people who have an emergency if they don't know what to do.

So here we go. You are about to learn what to do about all those things we talked about, and how to act like a *Junior Paramedic* if an emergency happens.

What should you do if you get cut by glass or by something sharp?

First, we have to stop the bleeding. Sometimes the bleeding from a cut isn't very bad, it just drips a little, and that sort of bleeding will usually stop all by itself. But if the bleeding is a LOT, then we have to put pressure on it with our hand to stop it right away, and we need to press down *hard*, that's called *"Direct Pressure."*

When you put direct pressure on a cut that is bleeding really badly don't take your hand off to check it, just keep the pressure on until a parent or EMT or Paramedic takes over for you. If you are putting direct pressure on somebody else's cut you should not get their blood on you, you should **first** put a thick cloth on the cut and *then* put pressure on top of the cloth. Sometimes we can get sick if we get the blood of somebody else on us, our *own* blood won't make us sick.

Make sure you have a thick cloth or towel over the cut and put pressure with your hand on top of the cloth or towel.

You could use a shirt folded over to be thick, or a washcloth, or even a few paper towels. In an emergency you can use your own shirt or the shirt of the person who is hurt, that's OK. In an emergency you don't have to worry about getting a stain on something or ruining a shirt, that's OK in an emergency. Your parents won't care if you ruin a shirt to try to stop a bleeding cut, you can get a new shirt.

What should you do if you have something sticking into you like a nail or knife?

If something is stuck into a person don't take it out, leave it in and don't move the thing or push on it. Just leave it alone and call for help.

What should you do if you might have a broken bone?

Until the doctor takes an x-ray at the hospital you don't know for sure what has happened, but if your or some other person's arm or leg is bent in a strange way where it doesn't usually bend, or if a bone is sticking out of the skin, then that is probably a *broken bone*, also called a ***fracture***. To fix a fracture the doctor will have to put a **cast** on it, and sometimes they might have to do an operation to help put the ends of the bones back together.

The first aid for somebody who might have a fracture is to just to keep the part that is hurt still, don't move it. If it's a foot or leg of course don't stand up or walk. Hold still and call for help.

What should you do if you get stung by a bee or wasp, or if you are bit by a dog or cat or some animal?

Bees and wasps or bugs that can bite can also cause an **allergic reaction**. Bites from dogs and cats or other animals can cause an **infection**. We should wash a sting or bite off with soap and then get to a doctor.

If a bite is bleeding a *little* you can cover it with a damp cloth or paper towel, if it is bleeding a LOT then you should put *direct pressure* on top of the damp cloth or paper towels and hold it that way until help comes.

What is an infection?

An **infection** is when you get too many germs in one place and they start to make poisons in your body. A doctor will have to give you medicine to kill the germs and stop the infection. You can sometimes tell you are getting an infection if a cut or scratch starts to hurt and gets red, it usually takes a day or two for an infection to start to hurt or to get red.

What is an allergic reaction?

Some people are '**allergic**' to peanuts, or to bee stings. People can be allergic to all sorts of things, even cats or dogs or dust. When they have an allergic reaction from something, like when they eat a peanut or get stung by a bee, they suddenly start having trouble breathing, and they might swell up or get puffy, and they sometimes get a red rash and start itching. People can be allergic to all sorts of things, not just peanuts or bee stings.

An **allergic reaction** can be very dangerous and someone who is having an allergic reaction needs to get to the doctor right away. There isn't really any first aid we can do that can help, we just need to call 9-1-1 right away to get them to the hospital.

What should you do if you bump your head and now you have a big lump there?

If you get a lump after you get hurt it's usually from some blood leaking under your skin, those lumps can get big and they can hurt. EMT's and Paramedics might call this lump a *hematoma*. You might be able to slow down the bleeding under your skin and stop the lump from getting bigger if you gently put some ice on top of the lump and let the skin get cold. A lump like this will go away but it might take a few days or even a week or more.

What should you do if you get dirt or sand in your eyes?

Dirt or sand in your eyes can cause a scratch to your eye. The best thing you can do is to try to wash the dirt or sand out of your eyes by running or pouring cool water gently into your eyes. Do that for at least a minute or two.

Even if you get the dirt or sand out it still might feel like something is in your eye if your eye has a scratch on it. The doctor will have to look into your eye with a special light that shows the scratches, and sometimes you'll have to have medicine put into your eye and then wear a patch over your eye for a few days until it gets better.

What should you do if you get burned by something?

A burn can be from fire or from something else hot, like hot water; most burns are that sort of burn. But you can also get a burn called a ***chemical burn*** from some sorts of liquids or powders. If the burn is from some liquid or powder you should wash it off with LOTS of fast running water and keep washing it until some adult or a rescuer takes over.

If the burn is from fire or something else hot you should cool the area with water. You want to make sure the skin on the burned part is cooled off, so it doesn't keep causing a bigger burn. After you cool it with water for just a little while you can stop the water. It will probably keep hurting, you won't be able to fix that, the doctor will have medicine to help take away some of the pain and make it heal. We should not play with fire or anything very hot and we should not handle chemicals we find, leave them alone.

What should you do if you have trouble breathing?

If someone is having a hard time breathing, they should sit up straight and someone should call 9-1-1. That's about all you can do. The EMT's or Paramedics will give them oxygen by putting a mask on their face, and then they'll get them to the hospital.

What should you do if you have a bloody scrape on your skin from falling down?

A scrape is also called an ***abrasion***. It's good to wash off any cut or scrape with soap and water and cover it with a clean cloth. You should see a doctor so that they can clean it off with special soap and put medicine on it to stop an infection.

What should you do if you get poison on you?

Many of the spray bottles, cans, and plastic bottles you might see in your house or garage are poisons. Some poisons are in bottles of insect spray or things to clean the bathroom or kitchen. You should be careful not to spill anything like that on you and you should not breathe in the smell of any of that stuff. These poisons can hurt your lungs and body and some of them can even kill you. If you get anything like that on you you should wash it off with soap right away. If you can smell something that might be a poison you should get away from it, get far enough away that you can't smell it anymore, and then go get an adult and tell them about it.

Don't EVER breathe in a chemical or poison on purpose, it could *kill you*. Spray paint and gas to fill lighters or bar-b-ques are *deadly poisons* that can kill you if you breathe them in your lungs. Those chemicals also damage your brain. If you hurt your brain it sometimes never gets better.

What should you do if your friend has a gun or a knife?

Sometimes someone will try to show you a gun or knife or something else dangerous. If that happens you should *get away* from them and from it quick, and go tell an adult. NEVER touch these things unless your parent is teaching you about it and tells you to touch it. NEVER stay with one of your friends or with anybody if they have a gun or a knife or something else dangerous, **get away** from them quick, and go tell an adult right away.

If you even *see* a gun you should think that it **<u>always</u> has bullets in it** and it can shoot if it is touched. Someone might say it's safe, because it doesn't have any bullets in it. A

14

gun should NEVER be pointed at a person! You should always **act like a gun <u>does</u> have bullets in it**, and is dangerous. You should NOT touch a gun or be anywhere near someone with a gun. It might have bullets in it but your friend doesn't think it does. ***You have to get far away quick***. If someone pulls the trigger or touches the gun it can shoot, and the bullet can go really far and hit you. You have to **get far away**, and go tell an adult. The only time it is safe to be around a gun is with your parents if they are teaching you about it.

What should you do if your friend has drugs or wants you to use them?

Lots of kids will have friends or people they know who have drugs. They might show you drugs and they might tell you that you should take drugs. You should get away from those people and go tell an adult about it.

Drugs can kill you, even if people tell you that drugs are safe, or fun, they are wrong, drugs are too dangerous to use. Some people will die the very first time they use a drug, even if their friend has taken that same drug and nothing bad happened. **Drugs are a bad idea**. Medicine from a doctor has a special job to do that can help the body, but medicine or drugs not given to you by a doctor can hurt your body.

Alcohol is a drug. Cigarettes have *nicotine* in them and that is a drug. *Marijuana* is a drug. There are LOTS of things that are drugs that have all sorts of other names, *ecstasy, LSD, heroin, speed, crack*, and lots and lots of other names.

Never take a pill somebody gives you, never smoke cigarettes or anything else, even the e-cigarettes that have steam and not smoke can have nicotine and other drugs in them. Some drugs are even on pieces of paper that people lick.

Most people who take drugs will tell you that drugs are GREAT, and they tell you it's fun, or that it makes you feel good, but all these drugs have poisons in them and they all have things about them that are bad for your body. **Drugs are a BAD idea**. You should stay away from people or friends that use drugs and get new friends that don't use drugs.

If you get in trouble for drugs you might not be able to get a job as an EMT or Paramedic, or as a Fire Fighter or Police Officer. Drugs are NOT for smart people, smart people know that drugs are a BAD idea and they don't use them.

YOU are a smart person and YOU have good common sense.

∞

Ok, you've learned a lot. It's time for the Junior Paramedic test. Think about what you've learned and pick the best answer for each question. Have your parents help you when you're done to make sure you got all the right answers.

The Official
Junior Paramedic Test

You must get ALL of these 15 questions right to pass this test.

If you miss a question go back to that page and read about it again, and make sure you know the right answer, then read the question again and mark the right answer.

When you know the right answers to ALL these questions you earn your Official Junior Paramedic card!

1. What is the very first thing you should do in an emergency? (Page 6)

(Pick ONE answer)

□ Stop any bleeding
□ Call 9-1-1
□ Make sure YOU are safe

2. How can you stop really bad bleeding? (Page 9)

(Pick ONE answer)

□ With a Band-Aid
□ By calling 9-1-1
□ By putting strong pressure on the cut

3. Some kid you know has a gun. What should you do FIRST? (Page 14)

(Pick ONE answer)

□ Call 9-1-1
□ Get FAR AWAY from it and from them, run and tell an adult
□ Take it away from them

4. You fell down on your bike. Your arm is bent in a strange way and it really hurts. What should you do? (Page 10)

(Pick ONE answer)

□ Try to move it
□ Hold very still while you wait for help

5. You got boiling hot water on you, what should you do? (Page 13)

(Pick ONE answer)

□ Put lots of cool water on your skin
□ Cry or scream for 5 minutes
□ Put Direct Pressure on it

6. You bumped your head and have a big lump on it. What should you do? (Page 12)

(Pick ONE answer)

☐ Put ice on it
☐ Start to cry
☐ Wash it with soap and water

7. When you get hurt is it OK to cry? (Page 4-5)

(Pick ONE answer)

☐ Yes, that's normal, but make sure you do your Junior Paramedic work right away, just crying won't fix the problem
☐ No, screaming is better than crying
☐ No, you shouldn't cry when you get hurt

8. Someone you know is using drugs, what should you do? (Page 15)

(Pick ONE answer)

☐ Use some too
☐ Get away from them and tell an adult
☐ Don't use any but you can still hang out with them

9. If something sharp is poked into you, what should you do? (Page 10)

(Pick ONE answer)

☐ Take it out
☐ Leave it in and go get help
☐ Put Direct Pressure on it

10. If a dog is wagging its tail you can pet it, it won't bite. Is that true? (Page 5)

(Pick ONE answer)

☐ No, you never know if a dog will bite, don't pet strange dogs
☐ Yes, it is true, wagging their tail means they are friendly and won't bite

11. Is this true? You should never call 9-1-1, only adults should do that. (Page 6)

(Pick ONE answer)

☐ That is true, 9-1-1 if only for adults
☐ That is NOT true, in an emergency anyone can call 9-1-1, even kids

12. If you had some emergency and no adult was around, what would you do? (Page 5 and 6)

(Pick ONE answer)

☐ Call a friend
☐ Call 9-1-1
☐ Just wait for an adult

13. What is an emergency? (Page 3)

(Pick all the answers that are true)

☐ An emergency is when something is wrong and you need help right away
☐ An emergency is a fire
☐ An emergency is when you need the police
☐ An emergency is when you need an ambulance
☐ Those things are ALL emergencies

14. The best way to get help in an emergency is to do what? (Page 5 and 6)

(Pick ONE answer)

☐ Call a friend
☐ Call 9-1-1
☐ Run around and cry

15. What does a Junior Paramedic know how to do?
(Page 6, 9, 12, 13, 14, 15)

(Pick all the answers that are true)

☐ A Junior Paramedic knows how to stay safe and calm in an emergency and to get help
☐ A Junior Paramedic knows how stop a cut from bleeding
☐ A Junior Paramedic knows how to cool off burned skin
☐ A Junior Paramedic knows what to do if someone has a gun or drugs
☐ A Junior Paramedic knows ALL those things

The end of the test

Ok, have your parents help check your test, and see if you got the right answers.

Did you pass the test?

If you missed any questions go back and study that page, and make sure you do know the right answer.

When you know the right answer you can go back and mark the right answer on the test, and then you got that question right. You have to have the right answer to all the questions to earn your Junior Paramedic Card.

Your Official Junior Paramedic Card.

Here's your *Official Junior Paramedic* card.

Congratulations!

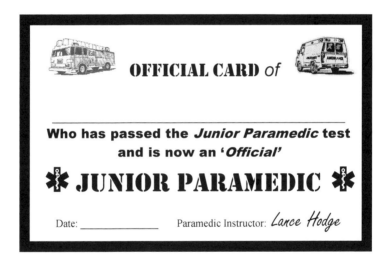

Carefully cut this card out on the *outside* edge, leaving some of the black border.
Have your parents write your first and last name on the card and the date, and then get the card laminated so that the card will last a long time.

Tell your friends about this book and about how they can become a *Junior Paramedic*.

Don't forget...

If an emergency happens YOU can call 9-1-1 to get help, and if it's safe to do it YOU can help.

If something bad is happening to you but you don't know what to do about it, don't stay quiet, don't keep a secret about something that you know is wrong, you should call 9-1-1, they can get someone to help you, no matter what the problem is.

Remember to try to be a *leader*, don't just follow, think for yourself, make good decisions, and when you know something is wrong, or dangerous, do the right thing and **don't do it**, and get away from it!

Be safe, and be smart, and use good common sense!

Congratulations on becoming a
Junior Paramedic!

(Here are some other books you might like to read)

Children's Books:

The Dream Writer, By Lance Hodge
ISBN-10: 1500616648   ISBN-13: 978-1500616649

Hannah's BIG Dream, By Lance Hodge
ISBN-10: 1500818720   ISBN-13: 978-1500818722

Lost in the woods, By Lance Hodge
ISBN-10: 1503264920   ISBN-13: 978-1503264922

Two Christmas Stories:
The Cookie that ate EVERYTHING
and Boy L-26 and his box of real magic tricks
ISBN-10: 1503279693   ISBN-13: 978-1503279698

Other Books for adults:

A Paramedic's Guide: Wilderness First Aid, By Lance Hodge
ISBN-10: 1500182664   ISBN-13: 978-1500182663

Topics, By Lance Hodge
ISBN-10: 1495253554   ISBN-13: 978-1495253553

The Oracle of Chadwick County, By Lance Hodge
ISBN-10: 1494943069   ISBN-13: 978-1494943066

Dexter Doubletree: The Book of Wonders, By Lance Hodge
ISBN-10: 1496064992   ISBN-13: 978-1496064998

The Thing in the Dark who lives under the bed, By Lance Hodge
ISBN-10: 1499615221   ISBN-13: 978-1499615227

The Writer, By Lance Hodge
ISBN-10: 1494997835   ISBN-13: 978-1494997830

Secrets of my Grandfather: A guide to Life's Wisdom,
By Lance Hodge ISBN-10: 1495204642   ISBN-13: 978-1495204647

Simple Zen, By Lance Hodge
ISBN-10: 1495258211   ISBN-13: 978-1495258213

Dexter Doubletree: The Curious Case of Laura Dunning,
By Lance Hodge ISBN-10: 1496141016   ISBN-13: 978-1496141019

Dexter Doubletree: The Case of The Brass Monkey, By Lance Hodge
ISBN-10: 1496153480   ISBN-13: 978-1496153487

Dexter Doubletree: "Bueller, Bueller…", By Lance Hodge
ISBN-10: 1496193350   ISBN-13: 978-1496193353

Dexter Doubletree: Four Cases and a Phone Call, By Lance Hodge
ISBN-10: 1497489334   ISBN-13: 978-1497489332

Dexter Doubletree: The End of the Line, By Lance Hodge
ISBN-10: 149952594X   ISBN-13: 978-1499525946

The Master Works: ART, By Lance Hodge
ISBN-10: 1499721463   ISBN-13: 978-1499721461

The Master Works: Art 2, By Lance Hodge
ISBN-10: 1500166448   ISBN-13: 978-1500166441

Seven Moons, By Lance Hodge
ISBN-10: 1500261114   ISBN-13: 978-1500261115

Poetry, Thirty Seven Years, By Lance Hodge
ISBN-10: 1495237532   ISBN-13: 978-1495237539

*For other titles search "Lance Hodge" on Amazon, Booksamillion,
Barnes & Noble, and other fine book sellers.*